The Midwife's Story

Meditations for Advent Times

Other Northstone books by Nancy Reeves

A Path Through Loss

I'd Say Yes, God, If I Knew What You Wanted

Found Through Loss

THE
Midwife's Story

Meditations for Advent Times

NANCY REEVES

WOODCUTS BY MARGARET KYLE

Northstone

Editor: Michael Schwartzentruber
Cover/design/illustrations: Margaret Kyle
Proofreading: Dianne Greenslade

Northstone Publishing acknowledges the financial
support of the Government of Canada through the
Book Publishing Industry Development Program for
its publishing activities.

Northstone Publishing is an imprint of WOOD LAKE
BOOKS INC., an employee-owned company, and
is committed to caring for the environment and all
creation. Northstone recycles and reuses and encourages
readers to do the same. Resources are printed on recycled
paper and more environmentally friendly groundwood
papers (newsprint), whenever possible. The trees used are
replaced through donations to the Scoutrees For Canada
Program. A portion of all profit is donated to charitable
organizations.

**National Library of Canada
Cataloguing in Publication Data**

Reeves, Nancy Christine, 1952-
 The midwife's story: meditations for
Advent times / Nancy Reeves; illustrations by
Margaret Kyle.

 ISBN 1-896836-59-3
 1. Advent–Poetry. 2. Advent–Meditations.
I. Title.
PS8585.E4447M52 2003   C811'.6
C2003-910726-4
PR9199.4.R44M52 2003

Published by Northstone Publishing,
an imprint of Wood Lake Books Inc.
Kelowna, British Columbia, Canada
www.joinhands.com

Printed in Canada at
Transcontinental Printing

CONTENTS

PART ONE

Introduction

HOW THE POEM &
ART CAME TO BE

It was Advent 1998. During my evening prayer time on December 17, I found myself watching in my mind's eye as a weary couple, the woman hugely pregnant, entered a town and began to look for lodging. I remembered my own pregnancy, 16 years earlier. During my last month, I was unable to walk down a street without some stranger stopping me, asking a question about my due date, giving unsolicited advice, speaking of their own pregnancy or, sometimes, even patting my belly. Pregnant women seem to be public property.

As I "watched" Mary and Joseph enter Bethlehem, I realized that even during the darkest hours, when most folks are asleep, there are some who are awake. Those who work during the night hours, a parent with an ill child, an elder with arthritis, young lovers – these people would probably have watched with interest as a heavily pregnant woman rode past.

Human nature is the same now as it was 2,000 years ago. The young couple would likely have been given blessings, questions, and advice. "When are you due?" "Is it your first?" "A little warmed wine will help a fretting baby." "Let me tell you where the midwife lives."

That last statement stopped my thoughts and opened my heart: "Midwife." Yes, of course there would be a midwife. Mary and Joseph were probably given explicit instructions by their families back home about what to do if the labor pains began while they were on their journey. A baby's birth is too precious and important to be unplanned.

So why wasn't the midwife mentioned? When we tell the stories of our experiences, we include the information that seems most important to us. Many details are left out. In speaking to a third person about a meal I shared with you, I might relate the menu and the decorations in the room, while you might recount our conversation. The midwife may not have been mentioned for a number of reasons; perhaps the storyteller didn't see her as important, or perhaps her presence would simply have been assumed and therefore the storyteller felt no need to speak of it.

In any event, I went to sleep that night wondering about the midwife's experience. At 3:30 a.m., I woke with the complete poem in my head. It wouldn't let me go, so after about 20 minutes, I turned on my computer and wrote it down.

Since writing the poem, a growing number of individuals and church groups have asked for copies. The poem contains many images and I frequently received requests to make it into a booklet, with each of the eight segments taking up one page, so that the imagery could be savored more effectively. To make it even richer, I wanted the poem to be illustrated. I approached an artist whose work I love. The idea of using a woodcut style appealed to both of us because woodcuts have a rough, unpolished feel – appropriate for a birthing story that was neither easy nor sterile. I hope you enjoy our collaborative effort.

WHAT IS ADVENT?

Many cultures and religions have a time of preparing body, mind, and spirit for an important event, particularly for a holy date. Advent, the four weeks before December 25, is the time Christians prepare for the celebration of God's incarnation as Jesus the Christ. The word "Advent" is taken from the Greek through the Latin and means "to come."

"But the only preparations I have time for are the gifts, the decorating,
the festive meal!" Yes, it is so easy for Christ to get lost in this busy season. Traditionally, each of the four weeks of Advent has a message or theme. In order, they are hope, peace, joy, and love. By intentionally giving some time each week to readying ourselves spiritually for the birth of Emmanuel – "God With Us" – we give our faith an opportunity to become deeper and richer. We let the Christmas story touch us more fully, so that its message can live in us.

WHY HANDS?

As Christians, we are called to be the hands of Christ in the world. Hands help us leave the safe darkness of the womb, and then care for our new bodily needs. They also help with our emotional, mental, and spiritual needs: comforting, protecting, stimulating, challenging.

We are loved by a hands-on God, who came to us as a baby that needed our hands. As an adult, Jesus used his hands in many ways to show God's longing for our healing and growth.

Many people speak of their experiences with God in tactile terms. "I felt held in the palm of God's Hand." "I sensed the Holy Spirit's warm touch on my shoulder, giving me the strength I needed." "As I sobbed in my friend's arms, I just knew that Jesus was holding me too."

Many of Jesus' teachings and actions used simple images, images his listeners could all relate to – bread and wine, lost coins, water. When I talked to my friend artist Mary Southard, CSJ, about this book, she experienced a strong sense that using hands to illustrate the nativity story might allow the reader to enter into and "own" it

more easily. For, by taking this story out of the compartment in our minds that views it as "a tale of long ago and far away," we can allow it to help us with that which desires to come to birth in us.

PREPARING YOUR WAY

*And you, child, will be called
the prophet of the Most High;
for you will go before the Lord
to prepare [God's] ways,
to give knowledge of salvation to
[God's] people by the forgiveness of their sins.
By the tender mercy of our God, the dawn
from on high will break upon us,
to give light to those who sit in darkness and
in the shadow of death,
to guide our feet into the way of peace.*
Luke 1:76–79

Do you consider yourself a prophet? It's probably not an occupation you would list on your resume. Although God may not call many of us to a visible career as a prophet, I believe that each of us is a prophet – a person who reveals or interprets God's will.

Each of our words and actions demonstrates our beliefs and values. Frequently during the day we choose between peaceful or hostile words and acts, ones that will spread light or darkness. We make a statement by the ways we relate to ourselves, others, and all of creation. We can choose to be God's messengers of hope, healing, and love, whether we are seeking to find a resolution to a conflict about vacation times at work, or supporting a friend struggling with alcoholism.

We can also be a prophet to ourselves. Within each of us lie areas of darkness and negativity, to which God longs to bring healing and light.

For example, even though we may have lots of evidence that we are intelligent or successful, the childhood message "You'll never amount to anything" may still have a grip on us.

USING THIS BOOK

I invite you to journey through this Advent season preparing yourself to become a more intentional revealer of God's will. The basic question for this trip is, "What healing and/or growth does God want to bring to birth in me?" Some methods to allow this book to support, guide, and challenge you on this journey are listed below.

1. Stay with the poem and pictures – For some, the poem and the pictures will be a jumping off point for exploring a theme. You might find that opening your heart and mind to the poem and the pictures is enough to bring new awareness and insight.

2. Suggested theme – In the second half of the book, each poem section is repeated and an invitation to explore a particular theme is given. There are a number of questions that might appeal to you as a method of deeper engagement with the theme.

3. Scripture – The second half of the book also contains excerpts from scripture. You might find that these excerpts are useful tools in themselves for helping your process along, or you may find that they work best when considered in conjunction with the suggested theme.

4. Do it your way – You may have a sense that God is inviting you to a method of clarification and exploration that has not been mentioned. For example, reading this poem may remind you of another book that you have been meaning to open. You now feel a strong urge to read this second book. God often uses one experience to draw our attention to another. Be careful to discern whether moving away from this meditation is a call, or a tangent to avoid looking at a particular issue or being with God.

General Guidelines

1.The poem is divided into eight sections, two for each week of Advent. I suggest reading each poem section and looking at each picture daily for the appropriate half week. Alternatively, you may begin the book 8 weeks prior to Christmas if you want to take a week with each theme. Remember the poem/picture at various times during the day. Be receptive to the different ways that

God offers guidance: through dreams, other reading, in prayer or meditation, through a carol heard over the public address system in the shopping mall, via another person.

2. Pray or meditate with each section. There are many ways to do this, so I will list only a few.

- Talk to God about the section. (Leave space for God to talk too.)
- Imagine yourself in the poem segment either as one of the characters or as yourself, maybe asking a question. Make the scene as real as you can by imagining the sights, sounds, smells, etc.
- Focus on the picture, maybe moving your hands into the same positions. As they move, allow your hands to "speak" to you.

3. Journaling can clarify feelings and issues. Allow your writing freedom. One day you may feel an urge to answer the suggested questions; another day you may write your impressions of the poem segment or picture.

4. Be receptive to whatever healing and growth God is inviting you to. You may decide that it would be helpful to explore a challenging relationship, and yet you start receiving insights and "awarenesses" about a pattern of non-assertion. Go with the Divine flow. It may be that allowing your pattern to be transformed will have far-reaching effects, including helping the challenging relationship. If you have no clue about what God wants you to explore, enter the process with receptivity and trust. It will become clear with time.

PART TWO

Poem & Art
The Midwife's Story

Later,

when the tale was told by others,

I was not mentioned –

like many women and men in essential jobs,

taken for granted.

But the Eternal One knows.

For our God gave me the gift

to ease the birth.

He was like so many others;

you could tell it was his first.

Anxious to get back to her.

Love shining in his eyes.

That wasn't the only thing shining that night.

You didn't need a light;

the whole sky was aglow with one star.

I knew they were packing them in.

But to make a woman, ripe to bursting,

sleep in a stable!

Oh, well.

At least no one would grumble at

the noise and the smell.

Birth so resembles death sometimes.

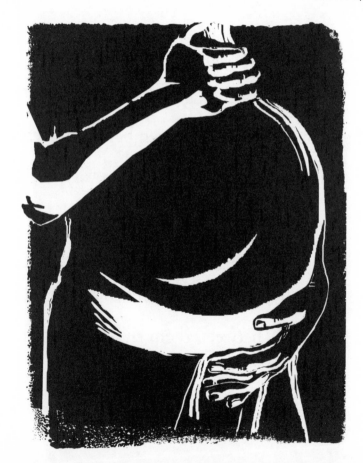

It was obvious she'd been prepared well –

far from mother, grandmother, cousin,

yet taught by them and remembering the teaching.

She knew that pain is part of every birth,

living with the hope and the joy.

He was a help too,

the strength and gentleness in his touch and look.

The love between them rivaled that star.

Then, the sweating and the pushing.
Hard work, harvesting the seed
planted months before and nurtured in darkness.
It's a willing sacrifice we make,
offering our bodies to be broken open
– water bursting forth, sweat and pain –
to birth a miracle.

They knew he was a boy child before I told them.

The final push was easy.

Sliding out of his warm nest,

he came

to be with us.

Little lambkin,

blood on his head.

Large eyes drinking in the world.

A person could fall into those eyes.

I held glory for a second,

then gave him to her – to them.

I was forgotten for a time, as is right.

Their baby-filled eyes

had no room for anything else.

They had a few minutes, the three

united in communion,

before the magnetism of birth drew others.

This time, men as well as women.

I'm not good with crowds and I felt full, satisfied –
my gift always ready,
prepared to make the way smoother.
I know I was inspired that night.
I left them to others and went home.
Grateful for my part
in bringing God to birth.

PART THREE

Advent Meditation – Suggested Themes & Scripture

WEEK 1A SUNDAY

GRATITUDE

Later,
when the tale was told by others,
I was not mentioned –
like many women and men,
in essential jobs, taken for granted.
But the Eternal One knows.
For our God gave me the gift
to ease the birth.

Any long or challenging journey goes more smoothly if we have packed things that help us on our way. In this journey through Advent, an attitude of gratitude will help us pack wisely. God gives us qualities that need to be honored and nurtured so that they can be used for our healing and growth. God gives us friends, teachers, counselors, and strangers who comfort, challenge, and speak words of truth to us. It is so easy to take our qualities for granted, saying, for example, "Oh, creativity just comes naturally to me, it's not a big deal." It is also easy to take the people in our lives for granted. By doing this, we cripple ourselves, making the journey more arduous.

Questions to clarify theme

- What qualities – such as perseverance, creativity, compassion – do you take for granted?
- How does this quality contribute to your healing and growth?
- What person have you been taking for granted? What gift do they bring you?

Journal or meditate

Over the next few days, express gratitude for these qualities or people. An attitude of gratitude helps us to be more receptive to how our loving God is present in our lives and it allows the transformative process to work more smoothly.

Scripture

A voice cries out:
"In the wilderness prepare
the way of the Lord,
make straight in the desert
a highway for our God."
Isaiah 40:3

෨

Offer to God a sacrifice of
thanksgiving,
and pay your vows to the Most High.
Psalm 50:14

WEEK 1B MIDWEEK

STEPPING INTO THE UNKNOWN WITH TRUST

He was like so many others;
you could tell it was his first.
Anxious to get back to her.
Love shining in his eyes.
That wasn't the only thing shining
that night.
You didn't need a light;
the whole sky was aglow with one star.

A ny journey contains unfamiliar elements. Sometimes it seems we are stepping into the unknown, which is totally beyond our control. Joseph had already been stretched past the familiar when he discovered that Mary was pregnant. Then he faced more strangeness when an angel came to him in a dream and asked him to accept Mary as his wife and the unborn child as his own. I imagine he felt he had all the newness he could handle. But then he heard he was to take his very pregnant wife on a long trip! The birth would likely come while they were far from home and from those who would normally provide support and guidance. How could he properly care for and keep safe his new wife and this son of God's? It would have taken a great deal of trust in Providence to step into this unknown, to do what he could do, and to do it with love.

Questions to clarify theme

(Pick one or choose your own.)

- What is currently changing in your life? What is your attitude toward this change?
- Look over the past year. How did you get here from there?
- Where is the newness, the unknown, in your life?
- How do you let God help you with the unknown?
- What beliefs do you have about trusting yourself, others, God?

Journal or meditate

Over the next few days, be aware of the times you are invited to trust yourself or another. Blind trust tends to be rigid and narrow; trust that clarifies and questions allows us to be more aware of life-affirming people and situations. It is best to cultivate this latter kind of trust.

Scripture

Her husband Joseph,
being a righteous man and unwilling
to expose her to public disgrace,
planned to dismiss her quietly.
But just when he had resolved to
do this,
an angel of the Lord appeared to him
in a dream and said,
"Joseph, son of David, do not be
afraid to take Mary as your wife,
for the child conceived in her is from
the Holy Spirit."
Matthew 1:19–20

～

[Joseph] went to be registered with
Mary,
to whom he was engaged and who was
expecting a child.
Luke 2:5

WEEK 2A SUNDAY

OBSTACLES ON THE WAY

I knew they were packing them in.
But to make a woman, ripe to bursting,
sleep in a stable!
Oh, well.
At least no one would grumble at
the noise and the smell.
Birth so resembles death sometimes.

When we agree to a change in our lives, to willingly accept the journey, we want the way to be smooth. Yet even if we've made reservations, sometimes there is no room for us at the inn. How do we handle these roadblocks on our way? Give up the journey? Use force to get ourselves the room we feel or think we deserve? Blocks are a part of life and because we have been given free will, God will not control our path. Our loving Creator will be with us, giving us strength and guidance to deal with life's challenges.

Questions to clarify theme
(Choose one or more.)
- What is currently blocking or challenging you? Ask the block what it needs, to be transformed.

- What is your usual pattern of attitudes and behavior when you encounter obstacles in your way? How do you feel about this pattern?
- Remember an obstacle in your past. How was God supporting and guiding you? If this is hard to see, look for God's traces by asking yourself, "Who or what showed me love, compassion, understanding during that time? Who or what gave me physical assistance or direction?"

Journal or meditate

Over the next few days, cultivate the qualities of receptivity (being open to God's presence in ways and places you are not used to) and patience.

Scripture

Do not be conformed to this world,
but be transformed by
the renewing of your minds,
so that you may discern
what is the will of God –
what is good and acceptable and
perfect.
Romans 12:2

᷍

Come to me, all you that are weary
and are carrying heavy burdens,
and I will give you rest.
Take my yoke upon you,
and learn from me;
for I am gentle and humble in heart,
and you will find rest for your souls.
For my yoke is easy, and
my burden is light.
Matthew 11:28–30

WEEK 2B MIDWEEK

FAMILY

*It was obvious she'd been
prepared well –
far from mother, grandmother, cousin,
yet taught by them and
remembering the teaching.
She knew that pain is part of
every birth,
living with the hope and the joy.*

*He was a help too,
the strength and gentleness
in his touch and look.
The love between them
rivaled that star.*

Birth does more than bring a child into the world; it creates a family. The experiences we have with our birth families, the families we marry into, and the people we come to view as family, such as a religious community or close friends, impact on us greatly. Also, every act of ours has a "ripple effect," influencing family, friends, acquaintances, and strangers.

Questions to clarify theme

- Who is involved with your journey at this time? How do you feel helped or hindered by them?
- What person in your family has had the strongest positive influence on you? How can you use this influence to assist your current process?

Journal or meditate

Over the next few days, reach out to members of your family. Let them know how they have influenced your life in positive ways; express gratitude. Let them know your current needs. Take time and care to clarify how you would like to approach those you feel are hindering your journey.

Scripture

For where two or three
are gathered in my name,
I am there among them.
Matthew 18:20

꿈

For this reason I bow my knees
before [our God],
from whom every family in heaven
and on earth takes its name.
I pray that, according to the riches of
[God's] glory,
[Our Creator] may grant that you may
be strengthened in your inner being
with power through [the] Spirit,
and that Christ may dwell in your
hearts through faith, as you are
being rooted and grounded in love.
Ephesians 3:14–17

WEEK 3A SUNDAY

PREPARING THE WAY IS WORK

Then, the sweating and the pushing.
Hard work, harvesting the seed
planted months before and
nurtured in darkness.
It's a willing sacrifice we make,
offering our bodies to be broken open
– water bursting forth, sweat and pain –
to birth a miracle.

Birthing ideas, attitudes, behaviors, and babies takes effort and is painful at times. Our society tends to view pain as bad – an experience to medicate away as quickly as possible. "Sacrifice" is also seen in a negative light, raising images of restriction, diminishment, suffering. The original meaning of "sacrifice" is "to make sacred." Therefore, anything we do to follow God's will is sacred and is a sacrifice. There is helpful and unhelpful pain, pain that is part of healing and growth and pain that harms or destroys for no creative purpose. By clarifying the type of pain we are experiencing, we will be more likely to respond to it appropriately.

Questions to clarify theme

- What is painful in your life right now? Is it helpful or unhelpful pain?
- How is your current journey sacred?

Journal or meditate

Over the next few days, make a commitment to allow transformation of unnecessary or unhelpful pain. Ask God's help. See your daily actions, and those of the people around you, as sacred.

Scripture

May those who sow in tears
reap with shouts of joy.
Those who go out weeping,
bearing the seed for sowing,
shall come home with shouts of joy,
carrying their sheaves.
Psalm 126:5–6

᎒

I appeal to you therefore,
brothers and sisters,
by the mercies of God,
to present your bodies as a living
sacrifice, holy and acceptable to God,
which is your spiritual worship.
Romans 12:1

WEEK 3B MIDWEEK

LAMB IN A STABLE – LAMB ON A CROSS

*They knew he was a boy child
before I told them.
The final push was easy.
Sliding out of his warm nest,
he came
to be with us.
Little lambkin,
blood on his head.
Large eyes drinking in the world.
A person could fall into those eyes.*

Good Friday and Christmas Day are important days in the Christian calendar. The cross of Good Friday and the manger of Christmas are both potent symbols of faith. Christ's birth and death are inseparable: the little "lambkin" in the manger is the Lamb of God.

Questions to clarify theme
- What images of Christ are helpful to you on your journey?
- With every new beginning, something dies or is changed. How is this occurring in your life right now?

Journal or meditate
Over the next few days, when you think of God at this time, what image(s) speak most loudly (e.g., Shepherd, Father,

Mother, Holy Midwife)? What image fits you as seeker at this time? Explore how the images of your spirituality inform and guide your way.

Scripture

And she gave birth to her firstborn son
and wrapped him in bands of cloth,
and laid him in a manger,
because there was no place for them
in the inn.
Luke 2:7

ॐ

The next day John [the Baptist] again
was standing with two of his disciples,
and as he watched Jesus walk by,
he exclaimed, "Look, here is
the Lamb of God."
John 1:35–36

ॐ

[Jesus] said to them,
"This is my blood of the covenant,
which is poured out for many."
Mark 14:24

ॐ

But when they came to Jesus and saw
that he was already dead,
they did not break his legs.
Instead, one of the soldiers pierced
his side with a spear,
and at once blood and
water came out.
John 19:33–34

WEEK 4A SUNDAY

SAVORING THE BIRTH

I held glory for a second,
then gave him to her – to them.
I was forgotten for a time, as is right.
Their baby-filled eyes
had no room for anything else.
They had a few minutes, the three
united in communion, before the
magnetism of birth drew others.
This time, men as well as women.

Once a task has been completed, do you spend a bit of time savoring what you have accomplished, or do you rush off to the next job? Taking time to acknowledge, rejoice in, and give thanks for an insight, awareness, or completed task has psychological as well as spiritual benefits. Remembering your process will make it easier to do it again when needed. Feelings of satisfaction can benefit self-image and self-esteem. Identifying the abilities we used in the process of developing the idea or task can deepen our relationship with our Creator. For we have been made in God's image, with love. Resting after completion also enables us to gracefully disengage from the idea or task and allows it to go where it needs to, such as into the care of another person.

Questions to clarify theme

- What is your pattern of thought and behavior after birthing an idea or task? How do you feel about this pattern?
- Remember a recently completed idea or task. Rejoice in it, give thanks for it, and rest with it for a few minutes. What is that experience like?

Journal or meditate

Over the next few days, be aware of completed ideas and tasks. Spend a few minutes savoring and resting.

Scripture

God saw everything
that [God] had made,
and indeed, it was very good…
And on the seventh day God finished
the work that [God] had done,
and [Our Creator] rested on
the seventh day…
Genesis 1:31 and 2:2

ॐ

By [God's] great mercy [we have been given] a new birth into a living hope through the resurrection of Jesus Christ from the dead, and into an inheritance that is imperishable, undefiled, and unfading.
1 Peter 1:3–4

WEEK 4B MIDWEEK

GIFTS HELP
PREPARE THE WAY

*I'm not good with crowds and
I felt full, satisfied –
my gift always ready,
prepared to make the way smoother.
I know I was inspired that night.
I left them to others and went home.
Grateful for my part
in bringing God to birth.*

Christmas is nearly upon us.
Children and adults speculate
about the gifts they will receive. Our
greatest gifts, those qualities and
talents that make each of us unique,
were given to us by God prior to our
birth. It is our job to discover, unwrap,
and use them to help ourselves and
others, and to bring God's kingdom
to earth. This discovery is a lifelong
process because, as we mature, our gifts
will be expressed in different ways for
different tasks. May this Christmas and
the coming year bring your dreams to
birth and may the gift you are to the
world continue to grow.

Questions to clarify theme

- Choose one of your gifts, such as
  loyalty or efficiency. How has it
  changed and evolved over the years?
- What insights and "awarenesses"

have you gained during this Advent season?
• What is coming to birth in you?

Journal or meditate
Over the next few days, realize that all around you is evidence of God's gift of love. Rejoice and sing with earth and heaven.

Scripture
You are the light of the world.
A city built on a hill cannot be hid.
No one after lighting a lamp
puts it under the bushel basket,
but on the lampstand, and
it gives light to all in the house.
In the same way,
let your light shine before others, so
that they may see your good works
and give glory to [God] in heaven.
Matthew 5:14–17

჻

But each has a particular gift from God,
one having one kind and
another a different kind.
1 Corinthians 7:7

჻

Like good stewards of
the manifold grace of God,
serve one another with
whatever gift each of you has received.
1 Peter 4:10

჻

For it was you
who formed my inward parts;
you knit me together
in my mother's womb.
I praise you for I am fearfully and
wonderfully made.
Psalm 139:13–14

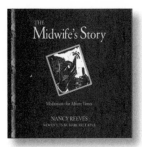